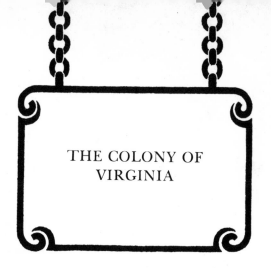

THE COLONY OF VIRGINIA

The Colony of
Virginia
By Dan Lacy

FRANKLIN WATTS, INC.
NEW YORK | 1973

Cover photograph (courtesy Charles Phelps Cushing) shows John Smith, leader at Jamestown, America's first permanent settlement. *Title page* (courtesy Charles Phelps Cushing) shows restored Governor's Palace, Williamsburg, capital of Colonial Virginia.

Other photographs courtesy of:
Brown Brothers–pp. 8, 10, 14, 20, 59, 60, 78;
Charles Phelps Cushing–pps. 31, 32 (by Sawders), 43 top, 45 (by Larkin), 64, 66, 69 (by Sawders), 73;
Culver Pictures–pps. viii, 26, 43 bottom, 51, 52;
New York Public Library–pps. 5, 22, 38.

Library of Congress Cataloging in Publication Data
Lacy, Dan Mabry, 1914–
    The Colony of Virginia.

    (A First book)
    SUMMARY: Traces the history of Virginia from its founding to its ratification of the Constitution of the United States in 1788.

    1. Virginia–History–Colonial period–Juvenile literature. [1. Virginia–History–Colonial period]
I. Title.
F229.L22   975.5'02   72-10780
ISBN 0-531-00783-9

CONTENTS

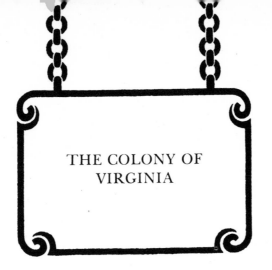

THE COLONY OF VIRGINIA

The landing at Jamestown, 1607

FIRST OF
THIRTEEN

If you visit Jamestown, Virginia, today you will find the still-standing wall of a ruined church. A great tree grows where the worshipers once kneeled. Nearby are excavated foundations of several small houses. If you go there when few visitors are crowding through the site, it will be very quiet. The James River will lap softly against the lowland, and you can look for miles up and down the silent stream and along the wooded banks.

At such a time, you might think yourself back through hundreds of years, to the evening of May 13, 1607. Three small ships, the *Susan Constant,* the *Godspeed,* and the *Discovery,* are anchored off the Jamestown peninsula. Even the largest of them is no bigger than a small modern fishing craft. It is hard to believe that 144 colonists are jammed into the little vessels. But they are an important 144 men and boys. When they land at Jamestown the following morning, they will plant the first English colony to survive in the New World. As they climb eagerly ashore, they will start the long train of history from which will grow the Commonwealth of Virginia and the United States of America.

Virginia was the first of the original thirteen English colonies in the New World, its charter dating from 1606.

Virginia was named for Elizabeth I — the "virgin queen." At first the name was applied to all the Atlantic coastal lands claimed by the English. Portions of the territory were given up through the years until the 1860s, when today's state boundaries were fixed.

From the landing at Jamestown until the American Revolution, the colony of Virginia played a leading role in the history and growth of the United States.

THE EARLY
SETTLEMENT

Englishmen had tried to settle in America before 1607. In August, 1587, Sir Walter Raleigh started a colony of more than 100 men, women, and children on Roanoke Island, off the coast of what is now North Carolina. But war between England and Spain for the next three years prevented Raleigh from sending supplies and more settlers to help the colonists. When a new expedition finally reached Roanoke in 1590, it found only an abandoned settlement. The word *Croatoan* was carved on a gatepost. No further trace of the colonists was found, and even today no one knows what became of the "Lost Colony."

The failure of Raleigh's colony discouraged further efforts at colonization during the closing years of Queen Elizabeth's reign. James I came to the English throne upon Elizabeth's death in 1603. By that time peace with Spain and increasing world trade had built up a wealthy group of London merchants. In 1606 they chartered the Virginia Company of London to establish colonies in the New World. These men hoped to gain a share of the riches that for nearly one hundred years had poured from the gold and silver mines of Mexico and Peru into the treasury of Spain.

The first settlers left England on December 20, 1606. They took the usual route of the day, following the steady trade winds southwestwardly across the Atlantic to the West Indies. From there they followed the Gulf Stream up the Atlantic coast to Chesapeake Bay.

The colonists had been told to find a place well inland, on navigable water but concealed from Spanish ships. After searching for several days they decided on the site of Jamestown. At that time, Jamestown, named for the king, was almost an island jutting out into the main channel of the James River. Ships could sail nearly to the banks of the river. Only a marshy strip of land connected the island to the mainland, and this could easily be defended by a barricade.

Jamestown island was beautiful in the Virginia spring. The great river flowing past was blue and clean, not muddy as it is today. The trees were in their first full green and alive with birds. After months on the three cramped little ships, the men came happily ashore and gave thanks to God. They thought they had come to a paradise.

But soon they were to learn differently. The first years at Jamestown were to be a time of hunger, suffering, and death. There were many reasons for this. The climate was far from healthful. Mosquitoes were everywhere, and most of the settlers were to suffer from malaria. Hunger, scurvy, fevers, digestive upsets from strange foods, and other sicknesses were to plague the colony. Most of the early settlers were adventurers ready to hunt for gold or explore, but not ready to labor in the fields to grow food.

Clearing the land for settlement

The Indians had heard of Raleigh's colony on Roanoke Island twenty years before. They knew the whites there had been cruel to the Indians and had killed many of them. But they knew, too, that Indian resistance had made Raleigh's colony fail. Perhaps for this reason they were hostile to the Jamestown settlers from the beginning, so that the English had to stay behind the walls of their little fort unless they went out in a large armed group.

The dangers and hardships called for a strong government, but, in fact, the government of the little colony was very weak. The Virginia Company had provided that the colony be governed by a council. The members were named in a secret document opened only after the settlers arrived in Virginia. The council could elect and remove a president, expel members, and add new ones. The president, although the supposed leader of the colony, had little more power than other members of the council. Weak and divided authority provoked quarrels among the colonists and among members of the council itself.

The colony was not abandoned by the Virginia Company. Each year it would send over ships with supplies and new settlers. But in many ways each new shipload would only add to the problems. The new colonists who came each year would rarely bring enough food for more than a few weeks. Most of them would soon become ill. Many would die and others became too weak to work. They would have to be cared for by the older settlers, themselves weak and hungry, and fed from the scanty supplies in the settlement.

That the colony survived at all in the first year is largely due to the courage and energy of Captain John Smith (1580–1631). He was a twenty-seven-year-old soldier who loved to boast. But he was also an experienced warrior and a brave man. During the worst times he ruled the colony alone because of the death

(6)

or illness of other members of the council. He gathered food, declared that no man could eat who did not work, kept up a bold front against the Indians, even obtained corn and meat from them, and still found time to explore the waters of Chesapeake Bay.

On one of Smith's expeditions, to explore the Chickahominy River, he had gone on ahead of his companions with an Indian guide. He was attacked and captured by Indians in December, 1607. The kept him prisoner until early January.

During that time, Smith became friends with Powhatan, the ruling chief over all the neighboring tribes, who belonged to the Algonquin group. Smith was well treated, but he said later that the Indians had intended to kill him and that his life had been saved by Pocahontas, Powhatan's young and beautiful daughter.

However, Smith's firm rule had made enemies in Jamestown. After he returned and was badly hurt in an accident, he was forced out of the council. He returned to England in 1609.

The following winter of 1609–10, without Smith's strong leadership, was called the "starving time." About 500 new settlers had arrived the previous August with part of their supplies missing because of a storm at sea. There was simply not enough food. People died daily, and those who lived crawled about to gather berries and acorns for food. The desperate colonists were even reduced to cannibalism. By winter's end, only 60 settlers were alive out of the 1,000 or more who had reached Virginia during the three previous years.

Just as the starving survivors were about to abandon the colony, a new group of colonists with supplies of food arrived in May, 1610. The company had decided to have the colony ruled by a single governor rather than by a quarreling council. Therefore, with the new expedition was Sir Thomas West, Lord De la

Warr (1577–1618), a respected nobleman and the new governor.

The colonists now stopped their bickering and united in an effort to save the colony. But they were still beset with illness and lived in daily fear of Indian attack. Lord De la Warr, or Delaware as he became known, was himself taken ill and had to return to England in 1611. But his deputies, Sir Thomas Dale and Sir Thomas Gates, ruled in his place. Dale, realizing the unhealthy location of Jamestown, founded a new settlement called Henrico farther up the James River, near the mouth of the Appomattox. A strong code of laws was issued, and a military type of discipline was enforced in the colony.

Two other developments helped to bring a measure of peace and security to the early settlement. John Rolfe (1585–1622), one of the colonists, married the Indian princess Pocahontas in 1614. Since Pocahontas was the favorite daughter of Powhatan, the marriage brought peace between the Indians and the settlers for the next eight years. Also, in 1612 Rolfe had succeeded in growing a mild form of West Indian tobacco in Virginia. The kind the Indians had been raising was harsh and could not be sold in England. Thus, Rolfe provided the colony with a new means to wealth. There was an almost endless demand for good tobacco in England, and soon the colonists were digging up the very streets of Jamestown to raise the costly weed.

The colony grew slowly but steadily in the following years. In 1619, for instance, 1,261 settlers arrived, doubling the population in one year.

There were two important groups among the 1619 settlers. One of the groups was women. Although there had been a few women in Virginia from the earliest years, almost all the settlers in the first harsh decade were men. Now that it was clear the colony would endure and that they would make their permanent homes in the New World, the colonists wanted wives and families.

The marriage of Pocahontas and John Rolfe

In 1619 the Virginia Company sent over ninety carefully chosen young women who were free to accept or reject any offers of marriage. These women were the first of many such groups to come to Virginia. (The first marriage in English America took place in 1608.)

The other group of arrivals brought a different kind of beginning. A Dutch trading ship landed at Jamestown in 1619 after trading through the West Indies. It was short of food, and offered about twenty black servants in exchange for supplies.

Many white settlers who did not have money to pay their passage to Virginia had come as "indentured servants." They agreed to work for a planter for a period of years, usually seven, in exchange for their passage to the New World and their food, clothing, and shelter. Apparently, the first blacks were also treated as indentured servants, scattered on plantations throughout the colony. Years passed before blacks were brought to Virginia in large numbers and before indentured servitude became slavery. But it had its start in 1619. The long and complex involvement of whites and blacks in clearing the land, working the fields, building the houses, and forming the Commonwealth of Virginia had begun.

Still another historic event marked the year of 1619. The London company was now controlled by men who believed in the power of Parliament in England. They thought the time had come to end the one-man rule in Virginia and to give the colonists a voice in their own government. Accordingly, they sent Sir George Yeardley (c. 1587–1627) to Jamestown with instructions to call an assembly. It would be composed of the governor's council, still appointed by the company in London, and a House of Burgesses, elected by the colonists. Two men, chosen by a vote of all freemen, would represent each separate planta-

The first slaves arrive at Jamestown aboard a Dutch trading ship in 1619.   (11)

tion or settlement. (Freemen included all adult males who were not indentured servants.) Voting thus became much more democratic in Jamestown than it was back in England and than it later became in Virginia. In England only owners or leaseholders of sizable amounts of land could vote. The same standards were later applied to the Virginia colony.

The first Assembly elected under these rules met on July 30, 1619. It remains the oldest legislative assembly in the Americas, and one of the oldest in the world. The Assembly could not enact laws contrary to those of England or of the charter of the London Company, and its acts could be vetoed by the governor. Yet, the Assembly did have an enormous role to play. Its very existence recognized that Englishmen in the New World had the right to take part in their own government just as did Englishmen in England. This precedent would be applied in each of the other twelve colonies as they were established. Thus, the House of Burgesses, and similar lower houses in other colonial assemblies, became the voices of the people in America. It was in those assemblies, created by Englishmen, that the ideas would be shaped that would lead to independence from the mother country.

In its first session the Virginia Assembly made only modest progress. It passed laws governing relations with the Indians, fixing prices for tobacco, requiring the colonists to plant mulberry trees (to get leaves to feed silkworms) and grapevines, forbidding drunkenness and gambling, requiring church attendance, and the like. But it marked a beginning on the long road to liberty.

After this high point of hope and prosperity, disaster struck again. In 1622, with the colony weakened by widespread illness during the preceding two years, the Indians attacked. Powhatan had died in 1618 and the new chief, his younger brother Ope-

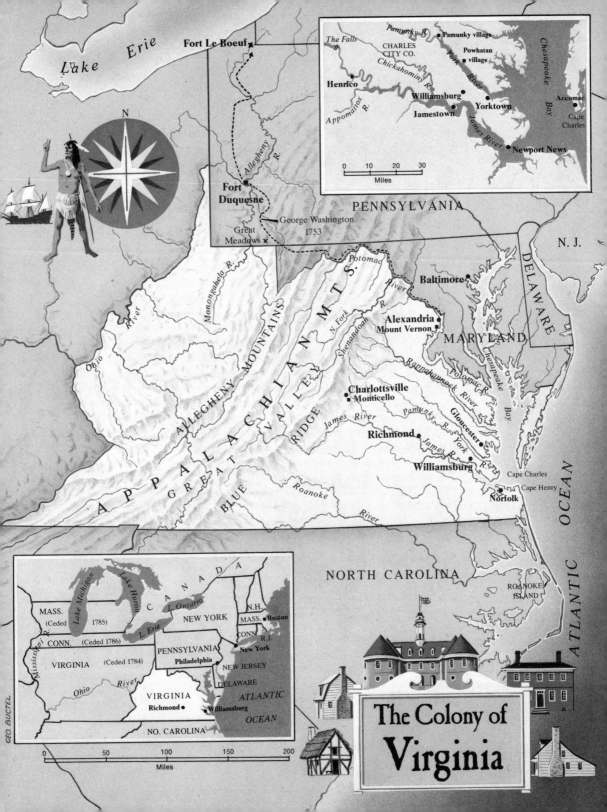

Lake Erie

Fort Le Boeuf

The Falls

Pamunky R. ■ Pamunky village

CHARLES
CITY CO.

Chickahominy R.

Powhatan
■ village

York River

Chesapeake Bay

Henrico

Williamsburg

Jamestown

Yorktown

■ Accomac

Appomattox R.

James River

Cape
Charles

● **Newport News**

0   10   20   30
Miles

N

PENNSYLVANIA

Allegheny R.

Fort Duquesne

George Washington
1753

Great
Meadows ✕

N. J.

Potomac River

Baltimore ●

DELAWARE

Alexandria
Mount Vernon

MARYLAND

Monongahela R.

Ohio River

APPALACHIAN MOUNTAINS

GREAT VALLEY

BLUE RIDGE

N. Fork

Shenandoah R.

Rappahannock River

Potomac R.

Chesapeake Bay

Charlottesville
■ Monticello

James River

Pamunky R.

York R.

Gloucester ●

Richmond

James R.

Williamsburg

Roanoke River

Cape Charles
Cape Henry

Norfolk ●

NORTH CAROLINA

ROANOKE
ISLAND

ATLANTIC OCEAN

CANADA

Lake Michigan

Lake Huron

L. Ontario

L. Erie

MASS.
(Ceded 1785)

CONN. (Ceded 1786)

VIRGINIA
(Ceded 1784)

Mississippi R.

Ohio River

NEW YORK

N.H.

MASS. ● Boston

CONN.
R.I.

New York

PENNSYLVANIA
● Philadelphia

NEW JERSEY

DELAWARE

VIRGINIA
● Richmond   ● Williamsburg

ATLANTIC
OCEAN

NO. CAROLINA

0   50   100   150   200
Miles

GEO. BUCTEL

The Colony of
Virginia

chancanough, hated the English for taking Indian lands. He had watched them spread steadily over the face of Virginia. Now he had a plan for their extinction.

On Friday morning, March 22, seemingly friendly Indian visitors appeared on more than 100 farms throughout the colony. Suddenly, the visitors turned on their hosts with tomahawk and arrow. Within hours 347 colonists had died.

Only a warning by an Indian boy, who told his white employer of the plans, prevented a much greater slaughter. As it was, Jamestown and the other larger settlements were able to protect themselves, for the killings took place largely on outlying farms.

But the damage went deeper even than the death toll. At first, frightened colonists abandoned their farms and drew back into the more thickly settled areas. Crops already planted were destroyed or abandoned. But the settlers soon began to fight back. Indian villages were burned and their crops destroyed in the field, condemning the tribes to hunger and starvation. Hundreds of Indian men, women, and children were killed. As a result, the Indians left the immediate area, and the colonists were free from attack for over twenty years.

But things were not going as well back in England. King James was becoming dissatisfied with the Virginia Company's administration of the New World colony. Proper care was not taken to choose people who were suited to colonization. Food and farming tools were not furnished in enough supply. So, for these and other reasons, King James cancelled the Virginia Company's charter in May, 1624, and Virginia became a royal colony.

Although John Smith, shown here during his captivity in 1607, was well treated, relations between Indian and settler had worsened to the point of attack by 1622.

(15)

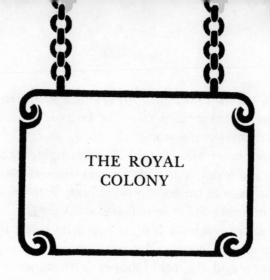

THE ROYAL COLONY

The government of Virginia did not change much as a royal colony. Now the king appointed the governor and council. James did not continue the Assembly at first, which alarmed the colonists. But the House of Burgesses was renewed in 1629 and it lasted until the Revolution.

Settlers continued to spread westward along the James and York rivers and north and south to the Rappahannock and Appomatox. In spite of the losses in the Indian uprising of 1622, the many hundreds who died in an epidemic the same year, and the continuing losses from illness, by 1625 Virginia's population was listed as 1,209 white men, 269 white women, and 23 blacks. Ten years later there were nearly 5,000 white settlers in the colony. They were fairly prosperous, abundantly supplied with food from garden vegetables, corn, hogs, poultry, and game. They were able to export tobacco to pay for goods imported from England. Roads were opened, and the forest was being pushed back. The colony had clearly become a permanent, even a flourishing, commonwealth.

In 1632 there was some concern in Virginia when Charles I, who had come to the throne upon the death of his father in 1625, granted the land north of the Potomac River to Sir George Calvert, Lord Baltimore (c. 1580–1632). This nobleman wanted to create a colony for his fellow Catholics, since their rights were limited by law in England. Virginia had regarded the land that was to become Maryland as part of its own territory. But in spite of this, and in spite of local conflicts, the Virginia authorities aided the first Maryland colonists, who arrived in 1634. As a result, the neighboring colony to the north prospered from the beginning and did not endure the suffering of Virginia's early years.

A new era in Virginia's history began when Sir William Berkeley (1606–77) became governor in 1641. Earlier governors had kept their roots in England. Sent over for a term of years to rule a distant colony, they had all considered England as home. It was England's interests, not Virginia's, that they represented.

Berkeley, however, became a Virginian. He acquired a large estate and built a great mansion at Green Spring, near what is now Williamsburg. He lived in the colony to the last months of his life. With one long interruption, he was its governor for thirty-five years. Although Berkeley was fanatically loyal to the crown, he shared the interests of his fellow planters and colonists.

However, the happy prosperity of the growing colony was harshly broken on April 18, 1644. The Indians, still led by Opechancanough, attacked again. Now an old man too feeble to walk, he saw one last chance to drive the whites from his ancestral lands.

The Indian attack was swift and well planned. But although over 500 whites were killed, by this time the colony was too firmly settled to be destroyed by even so bloody an uprising. The Indians were quickly and savagely defeated. Opechancanough was taken prisoner and murdered by a white soldier while awaiting trial. The new Indian leader, Necotowance, made peace in 1646. He recognized the king of England as his overlord, and granted the English all the rights to the peninsula between the York and James rivers, east of what is now Richmond. He agreed that Indians would stay away from white settlements. The colonists, in turn, agreed not to push into Indian lands. This agreement brought peace to the colony for more than thirty years.

There was no peace, however, back in England. King Charles was a rigid man, determined to uphold what he believed were the rights of the crown. Conflict developed between the rights of Parliament and the rights of the king. Finally, civil war broke out in 1642. It ended in 1649, when the Puritan forces — who wanted a simpler form of Protestantism — triumphed, and Charles was beheaded. A commonwealth was established, ruled by Parliament and headed by Oliver Cromwell (1599–1658) as Lord Protector.

The change of government had important results for all the English colonies in America. (Besides Virginia, there were now settlements at Massachusetts Bay, Plymouth, Connecticut, New Haven, Rhode Island, and Maryland.) Most Virginians were loyal to the king. However, a commission of four men was sent from London in 1651 to gain Virginia's submission to the new commonwealth.

This was arranged peacefully in January, 1652. Berkeley resigned as governor. The House of Burgesses was given complete authority over the colony. The new British government in London was facing so many problems at home and elsewhere in the empire that it almost completely ignored Virginia. For eight years, from 1652 to 1660, the colony was wholly self-governing, and the House of Burgesses was supreme. This experience implanted ideas of nearly independent self-rule that were never entirely forgotten in Virginia.

During those years the colony prospered. Expansion continued westward, as well as south of the James River and north of the York. Relations with the Indians remained generally peaceful, and trade between them and the settlers grew rapidly.

Oliver Cromwell died in 1658 and was succeeded by his son Richard. The son lacked the father's ability, and in 1660 Parliament called Charles II to the throne. The son of Charles I, the thirty-year-old monarch had been living in France since his father's execution.

The Virginia colony, always loyal at heart to the throne, was glad to welcome Charles II. Governor Berkeley was restored to his former position. But the period of Cromwell's rule had left permanent changes in Virginia. The Assembly did not resist when the king once again claimed the right to appoint the governor, or when the governor regained the right to appoint other officials. But it never lost the sense of its own importance. The sole power to tax Virginians, formally confirmed by the authorities in London, remained the Assembly's proudest right.

The next fifteen years were troubled times in Virginia. Overproduction of tobacco dropped prices so low that many planters lost money. The Navigation Acts, first passed in 1651, limited the right of Virginians to trade outside the British Empire and taxed their export of tobacco, producing further economic hardships.

Charles II showed little interest in Virginia and less understanding of its people's needs. For one thing, he gave the so-called Northern Neck, the land between the Rappahanock and Potomac rivers, to some noblemen who were his close friends. Naturally, the Virginians resented this.

Governor William Berkeley addressing the Virginia Assembly

Popular in his first term, Governor Berkeley became increasingly arrogant and disliked as he grew older. He tried to keep as much power as possible in his own hands as the king's representative. The people came to resent Berkeley, the colonial government at Jamestown, and their own county courts, in all of which they felt they had almost no part. Low prices for tobacco and economic hardship added to their resentment. During much of this time, England and the Netherlands were fighting an off-and-on naval war. On more than one occasion, Dutch ships sailed into Chesapeake Bay, and even up the James River. They destroyed ships loaded with the colonists' tobacco. This only added to the settlers' anger and sense of helplessness.

All this resentment came to a bitter head in 1675 when Indian warfare broke out again. After Opechancanough's murder, the Virginia Indians had remained quiet. But all along the Atlantic coast, the colonists were steadily expanding westward, pushing the Indians from their hunting lands, and the redmen were desperately resisting. The last great fight by the Indians of New England to save their homelands came in 1675 and 1676, and was known as King Philip's War.

In Virginia, tense relations exploded in the summer of 1675 with the killing of a Stafford County planter. White neighbors killed a number of Indians in revenge, including innocent members of the Susquehannock tribe. The outraged Susquehannocks killed more than thirty-five white settlers early in 1676, most of them along the upper Rappahannock.

The frightened whites demanded protection from the governor. The Susquehannocks asked for peace. Instead of an army, Berkeley proposed to build and man a series of forts in the west.

Most of the colonists did not like this idea at all. It meant heavier taxes for them, and they did not think the chain of forts provided any real protection. Many thought that Berkeley's re-

Raising tobacco in Jamestown

fusal to fight was due to the great deal of money he made by trading with the Indians.

Their resentment of Berkeley's refusal brought out in the open other reasons for the colonists' anger. Tobacco prices were low. Taxes were high and unfairly levied. A tight group of the governor's friends controlled the county courts as well as the government at Jamestown. Dutch ships continued to raid, and a disease killed off half the colony's cattle. The Indian hostilities, following everything else, were more than the colonists were willing to endure.

In April, 1676, the rumor spread that a large Indian war party was moving toward the upper settlements. An angry group of colonists in Charles City County came together to fight them. They had no legal authority and no leader. But they found one in a neighboring planter.

BACON'S REBELLION

Nathaniel Bacon (1647–76) was a well-born and well-educated Englishman with a likable and high-spirited nature. His reckless behavior had made his family think that Virginia might be a good place for him. He arrived in 1673 with enough money to buy a large plantation near the western edge of the settled area. His social status and wealth caused Governor Berkeley to appoint him to the council almost immediately, and by 1676 he was one of the recognized leaders of the colony.

Asked to head the small army, Bacon met the Susquehannock Indians on an island belonging to the Occanecee tribe, who claimed to be friendly to the colonists. The Occanecees fought and defeated the Susquehannocks, with encouragement and perhaps aid from Bacon's men. But as soon as the fight ended, Bacon's men attacked the Occanecees. They killed most of them, including the women and children, and destroyed their fort. The men claimed that they were starving for lack of supplies, had

(24)

been denied food, and finally were attacked by the Indians. Bacon's enemies claimed he deliberately attacked the friendly Occanecees to capture their large stock of beaver skins. Whatever the truth was, Bacon had struck a heavy blow against the feared Indians and was the most popular man in Virginia when he returned.

He was no hero to Berkeley, however, who proclaimed Bacon a traitor and called for the election of a new assembly, the first in fourteen years. Bacon himself was elected a Burgess, and the majority of the new House of Burgesses were friendly to him. The Assembly met in Jamestown in June, 1676. Bacon and his followers came in an armed sloop. Fearing he would be seized by Berkeley, Bacon slipped into Jamestown at night to consult with his friends there.

Berkeley's men captured him, however, and threatened to hang him. On his knees, Bacon assured the governor of his loyalty, and asked his pardon. Berkeley reappointed Bacon to the governor's council. At least that removed him from the House of Burgesses, where he might have been a leader of the group opposed to the governor.

The new Burgesses voted to raise an army of one thousand men to fight the Indians, with Nathaniel Bacon in command. But when Bacon heard a rumor that the governor would deny him the commission, he slipped out of Jamestown and rejoined his followers on the frontier.

His men shouted their determination to go back with him and demand a commission at gunpoint. On June 23, Bacon returned, and his followers, with guns loaded and cocked, surrounded the statehouse. The old governor, as brave as he was stubborn, marched out of the building alone to confront Bacon. He pulled open his coat and shirt, exposing his chest, and shouted: "Here! Shoot me, before God, a fair mark! Shoot!"

When Bacon refused, the old man started to pull his sword and fight him on the spot.

Bacon replied that he did not wish a killing but a commission. The governor yielded and signed commissions for Bacon and his main followers. The Assembly — freed of fear of the governor, and no doubt fearing Bacon and his men — now rushed through a number of liberal laws, all of which had one purpose — to break the hold over local government that had been gained by Berkeley and his friends.

Actually, the governor had no intention of respecting the pardon and commissions that he had given. As soon as Bacon and his men were out of Jamestown and marching against the Indians, Berkeley proclaimed them rebels and left the capital to raise an army against them.

Meanwhile, hearing what the governor had done, Bacon returned to the Jamestown area. He brought together most of the members of the council and had them swear to support him. He sent several ships to the eastern shore to attack and seize the governor, while he and a large group of men set off to attack the Pamunkey Indians.

The Pamunkeys, who lived in a great swamp on the northwestern edge of the settled area, claimed to be peaceful friends of the whites, and Berkeley had tried to protect them. Bacon's men insisted that the Pamunkeys had helped other tribes in their attacks on the colonists. The main Pamunkey village was destroyed, and a number of their leaders were killed or captured.

Governor Berkeley, across the Chesapeake Bay at Accomac, captured the ships and men that had been sent against him. This gave the governor control of the bays and rivers in Virginia. He immediately fitted out a little fleet and recaptured Jamestown.

Nathaniel Bacon confronts Governor Berkeley.

Bacon and his weary followers, just back from defeating the Pamunkeys, marched once more to Jamestown. Berkeley's men attacked, but fled under heavy fire and had no real heart to fight Bacon. Realizing this, Berkeley gave up the struggle, took to his ships, and sailed back to Accomac. Bacon set fire to Jamestown and destroyed America's first colony.

His victory was complete. The Indians were defeated. Except for the eastern shore, Bacon completely controlled the colony. Berkeley's power was broken. Many of the wealthier planters, as well as the frontiersmen and the poor, were now willing to accept Bacon as their leader. There was even a chance that the king might be persuaded to forgive the uprising against his governor.

But just at this time Bacon fell ill and died, not yet thirty. Without his leadership the movement quickly fell apart. Aided by the guns and crews of warships and armed merchant vessels, Berkeley soon defeated the divided and discouraged rebels. With only a pretense of trials, he captured and hanged their leaders and confiscated their plantations and farms. The rebellion was over.

Some historians have seen Bacon as an early fighter for the rights of the people, and even as a forerunner of the American Revolution a century later. But more recent writers have thought of him primarily as a frontier fighter against the Indians.

RULERS AND RULED — CONTINUING TROUBLE

Charles II knew that Berkeley's policies had been the principal cause of Bacon's Rebellion. He appointed a commission of three men to investigate conditions in Virginia. They brought with them a pardon for the rebels except Bacon (who was, of course, already dead) and a letter to Berkeley recalling him to England.

Berkeley stubbornly refused to return until he was forced reluctantly to sail in May, 1677. But he was already a sick man and died before seeing the king.

Berkeley's death did not end the oppression of the colonists and his successors did little to iron out problems between the rulers and the ruled. Finally, when the so-called Glorious Revolution occurred in England in 1688, it brought about change in the colonies as well.

The English Parliament, unhappy with the harsh rule of the Stuart kings — on the throne since 1603 — took the crown from James II, the Catholic brother of Charles II. They gave it to the former king's Protestant daughter, Mary, and to her husband, William of Orange, the ruler of Holland. A Bill of Rights was passed, establishing the rights of Englishmen and making it clear that even the king was responsible to Parliament and the law.

The Glorious Revolution brought greater freedom to the Englishmen in America as well as to those in England. Sir Francis Nicholson (1655–1728) was appointed lieutenant governor in 1690. He was a professional soldier, an able and energetic man who had previously been lieutenant governor of New England. In two years he greatly strengthened Virginia's defenses, improved its government, and restored good relations with the House of Burgesses. Nicholson was transferred to Maryland in 1692, but returned six years later as Virginia's governor.

During his first term, a college (founded 1693) had been chartered for Virginia. The Middle Plantation, about seven miles from Jamestown, in the "middle" of the peninsula between the York and James rivers, was chosen as the site. In 1696 the first building for the school was begun. It was called the College of William and Mary, in honor of the reigning king and queen. This was the second college established in the English colonies. Of the more than 2,000 colleges and universities in the United States today, only Harvard University, founded in 1636, is older than William and Mary.

The statehouse in Jamestown, rebuilt after Bacon's men burned it in 1676, was burned again in 1698. Since there had been dissatisfaction with swampy and malaria-infested Jamestown as the colony's capital, it was decided to build the new state-

The main building of the College of William and Mary. One of the oldest university buildings in the United States, it was designed by Sir Christopher Wren, noted English architect.

house near the new college. The name of Middle Plantation was changed to Williamsburg. Nicholson began the series of buildings, gardens, and public areas that today have been so magnificently restored as Colonial Williamsburg. (The capital of Virginia was changed to Richmond in 1779.)

In spite of these achievements, Nicholson's second term was not a success. He worked hard and he tried to organize Virginia forces to help England and the northern colonies against France in the war that was fought from 1702 to 1713. It was known in Europe as the War of Spanish Succession and in America as Queen Anne's War. (Anne, also a daughter of James II, took the throne in 1702.) But the people of Virginia resented his efforts to tax them for the war. He had also aroused the hostility of James Blair, the powerful commissioner of the bishop of London, and was recalled in 1705.

Restored gardens of the Palace of the Colonial Governors in Williamsburg

THE GOLDEN AGE

With the arrival of Alexander Spotswood as lieutenant governor in 1710, Virginia entered on the golden age of its colonial period. When Queen Anne died in 1715, leaving no heirs, Parliament turned to her distant cousin, George Louis of the House of Hanover, the great-great-grandson of James I.

George I was a German prince who was little interested in his new realm. He spoke no English, and often had to deal with his ministers in Latin. He was content to leave the government of Britain and the colonies to Parliament and his cabinet. It was not until George III, great-grandson of George I, came to the throne in 1760 that England again had a king who was determined to rule.

During this half-century, from 1710 to 1760, the ministers who ruled England in the king's name were generally willing to leave the colonies alone to develop in their own ways. The greatest of these leaders, Sir Robert Walpole, king's minister from 1721 to 1742, followed a deliberate policy of noninterference with the colonies, and welcomed their growing strength.

These were long years of peace for the Virginians. The Indians moved back behind the Blue Ridge and even into the Alleghenies, abandoning the rest of Virginia to the white man. For about thirty years after 1713 there was peace with the French. The British and French clashed again from 1740 to 1748 in a war known in Europe as the War of Austrian Succession and in the colonies as King George's War. But Virginia was little involved.

The prosperity and relative peace in England and Europe during those decades opened a wide market for tobacco and other products of the colonies. Business in Virginia boomed. Land was available for settlement to the mountains and beyond. The royal government, eager to extend the colony, was willing to grant land to ambitious speculators on liberal terms. The large families reared by each generation of colonists, and a steady flow of new settlers from Great Britain, quickly filled the empty areas.

THE
SLAVERY
ISSUE

Increasingly, as the years passed, a new kind of Virginian joined the earlier colonists. He was black and a slave. By 1660 the institution of slavery had been definitely established. Blacks were considered as property to be bought, sold, or inherited like cattle or sheep. As the colony grew more prosperous, larger and larger numbers of slaves were imported every year. By 1743 there were more than 40,000 slaves in Virginia, about one-third of the entire population. Many Virginians argued against importing more. By taxes and regulations, the Assembly attempted to limit the number. But as long as the great tobacco plantations remained prosperous, their owners continued to import blacks to work them, until their importation was finally forbidden by law in 1778.

The bringing in of tens of thousands of black slaves made possible a great change in the economic life of Virginia. Throughout much of the 1600's, most of the farms were worked by their owners and were no larger than could be cultivated by one man and his family. As a result, the building of the great estates of such families as the Carters, the Randolphs, the Lees, the Pages, the Burwells, or the Wormeleys, and even of such lesser estates as those of the Washingtons and Jeffersons, had to await the development of slavery. The magnificent estates, the elegant plantation homes, the kind of society that produced the great leaders of the American Revolution, were all based on the labor of slaves. Whatever they personally thought of the system, both George Washington and Thomas Jefferson were large slave owners.

By 1763 there were about 60,000 blacks in Virginia, almost all of whom were slaves. They made up half the population of the colony. Although until the Revolution a few new slaves were still brought in every year from Africa or the West Indies, almost all those in Virginia had been born there, as had their parents before them. They became highly skilled at farming and handicrafts. They not only cultivated the plantation fields, but also were the carpenters, masons, blacksmiths, cooks, butlers, coachmen, shoemakers, tailors, and general foremen on whom the life of the plantation depended.

Most of the slaves were surprisingly generous and forgiving in their attitudes toward the masters whom they supported by their labors. But the possibility of an uprising was a matter of constant concern to the white colonists. Many laws were passed providing that a slave could not leave his plantation without a pass, could not have firearms, and could not be taught to read and write. Slaves were forbidden to meet together unless a white man was present. They could not sue in court or testify against a white man. Owners of slaves were free to whip or punish them in almost any way they chose.

It was probably not often, however, that slaves were treated

Slaves tending the tobacco crop in colonial Virginia

with severe brutality, for a majority of planters were reasonably kind to their slaves. Most were fed, clothed, and cared for when they were old or sick. This was probably based not only on whatever kindness of one human to another the owners felt, but also on the fact that it is good business to take care of expensive property.

However, the slaves did not want to be well-cared-for property. They wanted to be free men and women, with freedom and opportunity for their children. This feeling burned deeply, even when slaves and owners were fond of each other, as they often were.

As the years passed, growing tobacco on the worn-out fields of tidewater Virginia became less and less profitable. Fewer laborers were needed, and slaves often became an economic burden to their owners. By the time of the American Revolution many white Virginians were unhappy about slavery and wished it had never come to the commonwealth. Some freed their slaves. Others said they would like to, but did not know what would become of them in a society that had kept them ignorant and given them so little opportunity.

LIVING IN THE
VIRGINIA COLONY

By the late 1600s there were already some large estates and wealthy families in Virginia. But it was in the half-century after 1700 that the plantation system developed to its fullest. However, it never included the majority of the people in Virginia. There were only two or three dozen families of really great wealth and a few hundred others who owned enough land and slaves to live in comfort without working the land with their own hands.

The families of great wealth had gained their riches not only by growing tobacco, but also by being successful merchants. Navigable rivers and bays reached deep into Virginia, so that seagoing ships could come to the docks of individual planters. For this reason, colonial Virginia did not develop young cities such as Boston, Newport, New York, Philadelphia, or Charleston, as did most other colonies. Instead, trade was carried on throughout the entire Virginia colony. The larger planters bought up the tobacco of their smaller neighbors and exported it to England. In turn they imported English goods and European wines, New England rum, and West Indian and African slaves, and resold them to lesser planters and small farmers. Some of the wealthiest owned their own ships to carry on this commerce.

Wealthy planters lived with great elegance. The rough homes that their predecessors had built in the early days of the colony were rebuilt in the prosperous 1700s. Estates like Brandon, Berkeley, Westover, and Gunston Hall were magnificent examples of the skill of architects and builders — spacious, beautiful, and lasting. Groves and avenues of splendid trees surrounded them. Furniture for the living rooms and dining rooms, silver, and china were imported from England and equaled the best in London homes.

There were many servants dressed in livery, and an abundant outpouring of food and drink in wealthy homes. Poultry, game, beef, pork, fish, and oysters were plentiful. Elaborate breads and desserts were baked in large kitchens, usually separate from the main house to reduce cooking odors and the risk of fire. Madeira wine, imported from islands belonging to Portugal, was a favorite, but there were also fine French and Spanish wines, rum from New England, and whiskey from Ireland and Scotland, as well as some that was homemade from rye and corn.

Great planters traveled with their families in large carriages or coaches drawn by two or four horses or on their own sloops. For recreation they hunted and raced their fine horses or drank and played piquet and other card games. At Williamsburg, when the Assembly was in session, there would be balls and plays and concerts. A few of the planters, such as Thomas Jefferson, were good musicians themselves.

But for all the pleasure and luxury, these planters were hardworking men. Running a big plantation was a very demand-

(41)

ing job in itself. Fields had to be cleared and decisions made as to the crops to plant. Tobacco was the mainstay, and it was a crop requiring careful attention at every stage.

The wealthier planters had much more to do than run their home plantations. Most of them owned several estates, with an overseer on each who had to be trained, given instructions, and checked on. The wealthiest planter of the time, Robert Carter, owned no less than forty-two plantations. Each had its own overseer. Half a dozen managers, each of whom had six to eight plantations under his supervision, controlled the overseers.

Just below these very wealthy planters with their great estates came a large group of more typical planters. They usually owned ten to twenty slaves, enough to spare themselves heavy work in the fields, but not enough to enable them to live in the elegant manner of the great families.

In the mid-1700s yeoman farm families still comprised the great majority of Virginia's population. They owned farms small enough to be worked by the family alone, perhaps with the help of an indentured white servant or one or two slaves. The husband and his children and perhaps his wife worked in the fields. Although they grew some tobacco for cash, their principal crops were corn, wheat, and vegetables for their own use. A few hogs, cattle, and poultry provided meat. Broadcloth or dress goods bought from a store might be used for their best clothes. But for every day the farmer's wife would spin linen and woolen thread from flax grown on the farm and from sheep raised there, and would weave the cloth and make the skirts and trousers and dresses herself. The tidewater area was mainly owned by larger

Above, Westover, one of the finest colonial mansions, ancestral home of the Byrd family of Virginia; below, Gunston Hall, home of George Mason

planters, but the piedmont area west to the mountains was made up for the most part of smaller farms. And it was the yeoman farmers who pioneered in the Shenandoah Valley and beyond, opening that vast region to settlement.

There were few really poor whites in Virginia. Although there were fewer indentured servants in the 1700s than in the century before, some young men and women still paid their passages to America by working as servants for a number of years. But most of them soon became landowners and independent farmers themselves. There was also more than enough work for carpenters, shoemakers, tailors, blacksmiths, and other skilled tradesmen. Families who had lost a husband might be temporarily destitute, but in a land always short of women, young and middle-aged widows soon remarried. Families were large, and people too old to work usually had children to support them.

A new flow of immigration came to the colony in the 1740s. Germans and Scotch-Irish (men and women of Scottish descent who lived in northern Ireland) had begun to pour into Philadelphia. They moved westward until they began to fill eastern and central Pennsylvania and flowed southward across Maryland into Virginia and North Carolina. Thousands of new Virginians settled just east of the Blue Ridge and in the Shenandoah Valley.

With the many kinds of new settlers came new religious beliefs. There were few Catholics or Jews in colonial Virginia, but there were many kinds of Protestants. The Anglican church (known today as Episcopalian) remained the official church of the colony. The Scotch-Irish were Presbyterians, and most of the Germans were Lutherans or German Reformed. Near the end of the colonial period the Baptists, and later the Methodists, began to attract thousands of new members.

Restored Williamsburg: a colonial woodworking shop

The Virginia colony did little for education. Planters educated their children at home, usually hiring tutors. Poorer farmers taught their own children to read and write and do simple arithmetic. Only the children of the wealthy and those intended for one of the professions usually went to school beyond the elementary grades. For those few there were academies in the colony, some church-supported, some run by a schoolmaster. The colony gave little support to the College of William and Mary, but it continued to survive as a small but important center of learning. A few of the wealthiest planters sent their sons to Britain to study law or medicine, and in general to get a polished education.

COLONIAL
GOVERNMENT

The most important figure in the colony of Virginia was the governor or the lieutenant governor representing a figurehead governor in England. He had a great deal of power. He was responsible for carrying out the laws and defending the colony; appointing other officials; presiding over the council when it sat as the upper house of the Assembly and when it met as the highest court in Virginia. Bills passed by the Assembly needed his consent to become laws. He was also the head of the Church of England in the colony. In all respects he stood at the head of Virginia society.

Opposite the governor stood the Assembly, with its elected House of Burgesses. All laws had to be passed by the Assembly. Only the Assembly could levy taxes and approve the spending of public funds. If the Assembly disapproved, the governor could not get money for any projects.

Voting was by no means completely democratic. Women could not vote, nor could blacks. Indentured servants and the few landless free poor could not vote. Even sons of well-to-do planters could not vote until they owned farms of their own.

Voting was not done by secret ballot as it is today. Every voter had to go to the county courthouse and publicly state his vote in the presence of the candidates. This probably made it difficult for a poor farmer to vote against a rich and powerful neighbor.

Local government was in the hands of the same planters who ran the colonial government in Williamsburg. In every county there were justices of the peace who together made up the county court, which tried important cases and governed the county. The justices were appointed by the governor, but he usually named whoever was recommended by the county. The little group that held power in each county could thus choose its own members.

It was not a political system we would think fair today. Yet the system did work. Planters perhaps were unjustifiably powerful, but they usually tried to use that power for the benefit of all.

Responsible planters were expected to devote a large part of their working hours to public service. They might be vestrymen in their parishes, justices of the county court, or members of the House of Burgesses. Although there was little or no pay involved, the planter could profit from a public position. He could see that the laws and the courts respected and protected the rights of men of property. If he got to the council, he had the opportunity to share in the large grants of frontier land as settlement spread westward.

This system produced a surprising number of thoughtful, responsible men devoted to the service of the people. George

Washington, Thomas Jefferson, James Madison, James Monroe, George Mason, Patrick Henry, and John Marshall, to name only a few, all gained their political training in this way.

CONFLICT WITH THE FRENCH

Virginia's charter gave the colony the lands not only west, but also northwest, of the original areas along the coast, and it extended all the way to the Pacific. No one knew exactly what this language in the charter meant. But Virginia used it as the basis for its claim to what are now West Virginia, western Pennsylvania, Ohio, Indiana, Illinois, and Michigan. Until the mid 1700s these claims meant nothing. But they became important as pioneers began to explore the areas.

Virginia's claims brought the colony into conflict with the French when France and Virginia claimed rights to the same wilderness. The goal for both was the point where the Allegheny and Monongahela rivers join to form the Ohio River (the site of

Governor Dinwiddie sends young George Washington on a difficult mission.

(50)

today's city of Pittsburgh). Whoever controlled that point would be in a strong position to control the entire Ohio Valley.

In 1753, when the French built a series of forts and connecting roads almost to present-day Pittsburgh, the British government became alarmed. It instructed the governor of Virginia to insist that the French leave the Ohio Valley.

Governor Robert Dinwiddie (1693–1770) decided to send a twenty-one-year-old youth on this difficult and dangerous job. His name was George Washington. Although a young man, Washington had a good deal of frontier experience as a surveyor and militia officer.

With a few guides and followers, Washington set out in November, 1753. He made his away across the mountains to what is now Pittsburgh and upstream to the nearest French fort. Finding no high-ranking officer there, he pressed on to Fort Le Beouf, not far south of Lake Erie. Washington was courteously received by the French officers, who made it clear that the French would not withdraw.

When Washington returned to Virginia, his message alarmed both the governor and the government in Britain. Washington was sent back to the frontier to raise a force and seize the junction of the Allegheny and Monongahela rivers. But before he could do so, the French took the area and established Fort Duquesne.

Washington tried to capture the fort, but was attacked by the French and defeated at a place called Great Meadows. He was allowed to take his troops back to Virginia and was not held as a prisoner of war.

Now Great Britain decided to make a major effort to cap-

The defeat of Braddock's forces

ture the fort. A large force of British Redcoats commanded by General Edward Braddock was sent from England. Marching from Winchester, Virginia, Braddock's forces plunged into the wilderness to retake Fort Duquesne. But they were ambushed by Indians and the French, and almost destroyed. George Washington was on Braddock's staff, and two horses were shot from beneath him in battle.

After Braddock's defeat, Virginia's frontier was open to the Indians, who were given guns and ammunition by the French. Governor Dinwiddie put Washington in charge of Virginia's soldiers. In hard, bloody fighting, he was able to push back the Indian attacks. In this way, Washington gained the battle experience he would later use in the Revolution.

What had begun as frontier skirmishes by the Virginia militia soon became one of history's great wars, known as the French and Indian War in the colonies and the Seven Years' War in Europe. It would involve the entire known world. The two great empires — French and English — would fight in North America, the Caribbean, India, Africa, and on the high seas, as well as in Europe itself.

Great Britain was finally victorious over the French in 1763. Yet it was, strangely, that very victory that would finally lead to the American Revolution.

LEADING TO REVOLUTION

Just the size of Britain's victory in the Seven Years' War gave it problems. Enormous new territories, including the Ohio Valley, had to be governed. A new method of ruling the enlarged empire had to be worked out. Britain had gone deeply in debt to win the war. Money had to be found to pay those debts, and to meet the cost of the army and navy that had to be kept up to defend the enlarged empire. The British felt that the colonists should help to pay those expenses. And that was the start of the trouble.

To help raise money, Parliament passed the Stamp Act in March, 1765. It required a stamp on every copy of a newspaper and on every official document. Courts could not be held, ships could not sail, taverns could not remain open, and no license could be issued without a stamp.

The colonists were outraged, nowhere more so than in Virginia. Patrick Henry (1736–99) was a young member of the

Virginia House of Burgesses at the time. Already famous as an orator, he gave a fiery speech against the Stamp Act. In fact, his attack on the king was so violent that members accused him of treason. His oratory won, however, and the Burgesses adopted seven resolutions. The first five only repeated, in stronger language, what Virginians had said before — they could be lawfully taxed only by their own representatives. But the last two resolutions went further. They stated that Virginians were not bound to obey any act of Parliament or other law proposing to tax them without the consent of the Burgesses. And they added that anyone who claimed that England could tax the colonists without their consent was an enemy of Virginia — a statement that called on Virginians to rebel if necessary.

The last two resolutions were later repealed. But the repeal came only after all seven had been printed and sent to the other colonies. The Virginia Resolves, as they were called, became the call to resist the Stamp Act in all the colonies.

Following Virginia's lead, the other twelve colonies simply refused to pay the stamp tax. Helpless to collect, Parliament repealed it.

But Parliament had not given up the idea that it had the right to tax the colonists. In 1767 it passed a law that would tax a number of export products from England — glass, paper, tea, and the like. These taxes would be collected when the goods were unloaded in American ports. The colonists would pay them in the form of higher prices.

Virginia was one of the first colonies to state its objection to the new taxes. A strong resolution of the whole Assembly condemned them as unconstitutional. When Virginia and other colonies refused to buy anything imported from England, the British government repealed the new taxes in 1769. However, they kept the tax on tea as a way of saying that they still had the right to tax if they chose to do so.

This problem came to a head in November, 1773, when colonists in Massachusetts disguised themselves as Indians, boarded an English ship in Boston harbor, and dumped its cargo of tea into the water.

Naturally, the British were furious. They closed the port of Boston and took away much of the governing power from the Massachusetts colony. Then they further angered the colonists, especially Virginians, the following spring by passing the Quebec Act. It took all the lands in the Ohio Valley claimed by Virginia and made them part of Quebec, the Canadian province seized from the French in 1763.

THE
CONTINENTAL
CONGRESS

After the Quebec Act, the colonies decided to get together to decide on a joint action. A Continental Congress met in Philadelphia in September, 1774. Virginia's representatives were Richard Henry Lee, Edmund Pendleton, Peyton Randolph, Richard Bland, Benjamin Harrison, Patrick Henry, and George Washington. It was the largest and most able delegation to the Congress, and included the leading citizens of the Virginia colony. Their presence made clear Virginia's determination to oppose any attack on the rights of the colonists.

The Continental Congress moved slowly. A petition to George III begged him to withdraw the acts that punished Massachusetts after the so-called Boston Tea Party. To give force to their protests, the Congress urged all the colonies to stop buying

Delegates leaving the First Continental Congress

anything from Great Britain. They resolved to meet again in May, 1775.

In Virginia the governor would not permit the Assembly to convene officially, so a "convention" elected by the people met in March, 1775. Patrick Henry was again the spokesman for action against Great Britain. It was there that Henry made his most famous speech, in which he shouted:

"Gentlemen may cry peace, peace — but there is no peace. The war is actually begun! The next gale that sweeps from the North will bring to our ears the clash of resounding arms! Our brethren are already in the field! Why stand we here idle? . . . Is life so dear, or peace so sweet, as to be purchased at the price of chains and slavery? Forbid it, Almighty God! I know not what course others may take; but as for me, give me liberty, or give me death."

Once more, Henry's oratory was persuasive. The convention voted to arm the colony, and appointed a committee of three to make preparations.

Henry was right about the next gale from the north bringing news of battle. Soon after he spoke, British troops moved out of Boston to try to capture some of the Massachusetts leaders. They failed and were driven back in disorder. But sharp fighting had occurred at Lexington and Concord in April, 1775, and many New Englanders had been killed. The war had begun.

Patrick Henry delivers his famous "Give me liberty, or give me death" speech.

(61)

THE FIGHT FOR INDEPENDENCE

Less than a month after the battles of Lexington and Concord, the Second Continental Congress met at Philadelphia. Again Virginia had one of the largest and strongest delegations. George Washington was appointed commanding general of all "Continental" forces under the authority of Congress. He resigned his seat in the Congress to take command immediately.

The first skirmishes of the war were fought around Boston and along the Virginia coast. During this time Americans were debating whether they should be fighting for their rights within the British Empire or whether they should fight for independence.

The North Carolina Convention, meeting in April, 1776, was the first to instruct its delegates to vote for independence. It was followed by Virginia on May 15. Since Virginia was the largest and most respected colony, its vote was the turning point toward independence. On June 29 the Virginia Convention adopted a new constitution, saying it was necessary because "the government of this country, as formerly exercised under the crown of Great Britain, is totally dissolved." This was really Virginia's own declaration of independence.

On June 7 Richard Henry Lee had introduced a motion in the Congress declaring that the united colonies were and of right ought to be free and independent states. On July 2 the motion was carried. Two days later the Continental Congress adopted the Declaration of Independence. It had been drafted by Thomas Jefferson, a young lawyer first serving on the Virginia delegation.

For the next three years the American Revolution was fought almost entirely in New York, New Jersey, and Pennsylvania. The British recognized New England, especially Massachusetts, and Virginia as strong revolutionary centers. Therefore, they concentrated their efforts in the middle colonies, the Carolinas, and Georgia.

After an American victory over British forces led by John Burgoyne at Saratoga, New York, in 1777, the French decided to enter the war as allies of the colonies. The British gave up trying to conquer the middle colonies and moved to the south. Both 1779 and 1780 were gloomy years in the south for the American cause.

For a while in 1781 the British controlled much of Virginia. The legislature had moved from Richmond to Charlottesville to escape the Redcoats. General Charles Cornwallis sent his cavalry on a swift raid to Charlottesville. Warned just in time, the legislators escaped. Thomas Jefferson, then the governor of Virginia, was almost captured in his home at Monticello.

Washington realized that the fighting in Virginia was now serious. He sent General Anthony Wayne south with a sizable portion of his regular army. Against this larger American force, Cornwallis decided to retreat to the tidewater area, where he could be reinforced by sea. He occupied and fortified the little village of Yorktown. He placed some of his troops at Gloucester, on the other side of the York River. There he waited for new troops and supplies that would enable him to conquer the whole Chesapeake Bay area. But a large French fleet moved up from the West Indies and seized control of the entrance to Chesapeake Bay. Until a new and larger British fleet could arrive, Cornwallis was trapped.

Washington saw his chance. His troops, and an even larger body of French forces, marched overland from near New York to the head of Chesapeake Bay near Baltimore, and were moved from there by ship to the peninsula between the James and York rivers. There they attacked Cornwallis. On October 19, 1781, the British commander surrendered.

The war was over. But the British still held New York, Newport, and a few other posts. It would be nearly two years before the king's representative signed a treaty at Paris recognizing that the United States were, in fact, independent, and months after that before the last British troops boarded ship to sail from New York.

But the long struggle for independence that had begun with Richard Henry Lee's motion that "these united colonies are and of right ought to be free and independent states" really ended at Yorktown on Virginia soil. It was only a few miles

Richard Henry Lee declared that the colonies should be free and independent states.

General John Burgoyne in a conference with Indians

from the site of Patrick Henry's fiery attack on the Stamp Act, which was the first clear statement of America's independent rights.

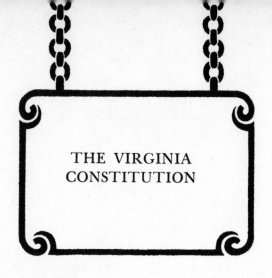

THE VIRGINIA CONSTITUTION

Virginia's new constitution, adopted in 1776, carried over ideas of the colonial period. The governor had always represented the power of the king, and Virginia had come to fear a strong governor. Now the governor was elected by the Assembly for one year at a time and had almost no power. All power was in the hands of the House of Burgesses.

Thomas Jefferson, among others, was determined to create a freer and more democratic society in Virginia. In December, 1776, the legislature had adopted a Bill of Rights, guaranteeing such rights as freedom of the press, of assembly, and the right to trial by jury.

But Jefferson wanted more. He began a long and only partly successful fight for his ideas. Two important laws were repealed

The University of Virginia, part of Thomas Jefferson's dream for the new commonwealth

(68)

under his lead — the laws of entail and primogeniture. Entail allowed a landowner to require that his estate descend intact through generations of his descendants. Primogeniture gave preference to the oldest son in inheriting the estate of a man who died without a will. Both laws tended to keep power and wealth in the hands of the large planters.

Next Jefferson moved against the harsh criminal law in Virginia. A new criminal code was adopted. Although it still seems very harsh by today's standards, it was moderate and enlightened for the times.

In 1779 the legislature ended the recognition of the Episcopal church as the official faith of the state. In 1786 Jefferson won approval of his cherished Statute for Religious Liberty. Virginians were free, as they are today, to worship, or not to, in any way they chose.

Jefferson failed in other areas, however. He wanted free schools for all white children throughout the state. The brightest would be given free scholarships to the academies, and the best academy graduates would be given free college educations. But his ideas were too advanced for the time, and the legislature would not act upon them. Decades later part of Jefferson's dream came true with the creation of the University of Virginia. But it was not until well after the Civil War that Virginia earnestly tried to provide an elementary education for its children.

The most ambitious of Jefferson's goals was the abolition of slavery. His plan would have provided for the gradual freeing of slaves, with payment to their owners. But white Virginians were not yet ready to think of liberty and equality for blacks. If Jefferson's plan had been adopted, decades of controversy might have been avoided. There might have been no Civil War, with its bitterness and destruction. But the chance was lost.

FORMING THE
CONSTITUTION
OF THE
UNITED STATES

Just as the new Commonwealth of Virginia needed a constitution, so did the new United States of America. While Thomas Jefferson's committee had been drafting the Declaration of Independence, another committee, headed by John Dickinson of Delaware, was drafting the Articles of Confederation.

The Articles of Confederation were not approved until 1781. There were two reasons for the delay. The main reason was that the colonists, anxious to rid themselves of the authority of Great Britain, were not so anxious to put themselves under a new authority — even one of their own choosing. The other reason was the question of how to apportion the western lands beyond the Allegheny Mountains. Under the colonial charters, some of the states claimed vast areas of the west. Virginia itself claimed a large part of the Ohio Valley. The states without claims to western lands argued that this territory had been won from Great Britain by all the states and should belong to all the states. They would not accept the Articles of Confederation until this question was settled.

Finally, in 1780, Virginia agreed to give up most of its claims. What is now West Virginia and Kentucky remained a part of Virginia, however. The other states with land claims followed Virginia's example, and the Articles were approved in 1781.

But the Articles of Confederation provided for a very weak central government. It had no power to tax or to regulate trade. It had no courts and no chief executive. The leaders of the American Revolution knew that a strong central government was necessary if the new country was to survive. At first they tried to amend the Articles. But since every change required approval of all thirteen states, nothing was ever accomplished.

In 1787 representatives from every state but Rhode Island met in Philadelphia. They formed what became known as the Constitutional Convention.

Virginia was a leader in uniting the states. George Washington, head of the Virginia delegation, was chosen to preside over the convention. The next most influential member was a young lawyer from Virginia named James Madison.

Virginia proposed what became known as the Virginia Plan. It provided for a legislature of two houses — the lower house elected by the people, the upper house elected by members of the lower house. Both houses would elect a chief executive. The legislature, or Congress, could levy taxes, regulate trade, and veto laws passed by the state governments.

Many delegates objected to the Virginia Plan. It gave too much power, they said, to the national government. The smaller

Modern Virginia. This statue of Captain John Smith faces the James River at Jamestown, site of the first permanent settlement in America.

states feared they would have no voice in a Congress where votes depended upon population.

Led by New Jersey, the smaller states proposed an alternate plan that would give equal representation to the states and less power to the central government.

Under the leadership of George Washington and James Madison, who had been the principal author of the Virginia Plan, a compromise was reached in September, 1787. A constitution was drafted, providing for a government as we know it today. The president would be chosen by electors. The two-house Congress would be comprised of a Senate, where every state would have two votes, and a House of Representatives, where the number of votes would depend upon population. The federal government would have its own courts. And the constitution would become the supreme law of the land.

TO RATIFY
OR NOT

The Constitutional Convention decided that each state must call a special convention to ratify (accept) the Constitution. As soon as nine states did so, it would become the law of the land.

Delaware was the first state to ratify. But many eyes turned to Virginia to see what it would do. Virginia was not only the oldest and largest state, but had also been a leader in the Revolution. A number of Virginians had been responsible for the contents of the Constitution. Would Virginia ratify?

The outcome was far from certain. Certainly Washington and Madison wanted to accept the Constitution. But men such as Patrick Henry and George Mason, a leader in the Revolution, were opposed. Thomas Jefferson, in Paris as ambassador to France at the time, was not at all certain that Virginia should ratify.

In June, 1788, Virginia held a state convention. Eight states had ratified the Constitution by this time. Would Virginia make it the law of the land?

The debate went on for almost a month. One of the most serious arguments against the Constitution was that it did not provide for a Bill of Rights, like those found in the constitutions of the individual states.

Finally, a compromise was reached. Madison and other supporters of the Constitution agreed that in the first Congress of the new government they would work for an amendment to the Constitution providing for a Bill of Rights. The convention agreed to ratify.

A NEW NATION —
A NEW STATE

When Virginia voted to ratify the Constitution, it did not know that New Hampshire had already done so. The Constitution was a reality. Thus, the first colony in the New World became the tenth state in the new nation. The remaining three states all ratified by 1790.

Virginia made one more important contribution to the new nation. When the first presidential election was held in 1788, every vote went to George Washington. On April 30, 1789, standing on the balcony of Federal Hall in New York City, Washington became the first president of the United States of America. (Seven other natives of Virginia later became president — more than from any other state.)

A new nation had finally come into being. It had grown in great part from the visions and labors of Virginians, from the first half-starved settlers of Jamestown and the pioneers of the West, from Patrick Henry and George Mason, from Thomas

George Washington in a triumphal procession on Broadway, New York City

Jefferson and Richard Henry Lee, from James Madison and George Washington, and from thousands of others — men and women whose lives had gone into the making of the Commonwealth of Virginia and the union of which it was a part.

BOOKS FOR
FURTHER
READING

Borreson, Mary J. *Let's Go to Colonial Williamsburg*. New York: Putnam, 1962.

Bulla, Clyde R. *Pocahontas and the Strangers*. New York: Crowell, 1971.

Davis, Burke. *America's First Army*. Virginia: Williamsburg, 1962.

Foster, Genevieve. *World of Captain John Smith*. New York: Scribner, 1959.

Gurney, Gene and Clare. *Monticello*. New York: Watts, 1966.

Ingraham, Leonard W. *An Album of Colonial America*. New York: Watts, 1969.

———. *Slavery in the United States*. New York: Watts, 1968.

Morris, Richard B. *The First Book of the Constitution*. New York: Watts, 1958.

Rich, Louise Dickinson. *The First Book of the Early Settlers*. New York: Watts, 1960.

INDEX

ABOUT
THE AUTHOR

Dan Lacy was born in Newport News, Virginia, and educated at the University of North Carolina, where he majored in history. He is the author of a number of books, including *The Lost Colony* for Franklin Watts, Inc. A resident of Irvington, New York, Mr. Lacy is married and has three children.

DATE DUE

AUG 30 73	MAR 5		
Mullen	SEP		
Mullen	SEP 21		
NOV 7	SEP 10		
SEP 21	SEP 22		
Meese	APR 8		
DEC 13	OCT 29		
APR 21	NOV 6		
Mullen	OCT 6		
FEB 10	NOV 15		
SEP 17	JAN 19		
OCT 4	King		
NOV 28	JAN 9		
DEC 1	JAN 16		
APR 13	Flan		
OCT			
NOV 1			
GAYLORD			PRINTED IN U.S.A.